ALONG THE UCAYALI
Pucallpa to Iquitos

By Frederick L. Kramer

To order additional copies of this book, contact:
Xlibris
844-714-8691
www.Xlibris.com
Orders@Xlibris.com

ISBN: Softcover   978-1-6641-4149-0
        Hardcover   978-1-6641-4148-3
        EBook   978-1-6641-4147-6

Print information available on the last page

Rev. date: 12/07/2020

To Leo
and
The Zamora Family
and
Mr. Thomas W. Hall, Jr.
and
to My Loving Family

I wish to thank Myles Ludwig, Professor of Memoirs at the Society of the Four Arts, Palm Beach, Florida, for his guiding inspirations in helping me write this memoir.

As well, I wish to thank Tina Russell, Melody Hillock and Eric Moser for their assistance.

Contents

CHAPTER 1

GRANDMA ROSE'S PEA SOUP

I didn't realize it then, but the life I would soon lead became like the Ucayali River, winding and meandering through various turns and twists, Fred thought. The Ucayali flows North in Peru for *mas o menos* 1,600 river miles and about 1,000 air miles. Eventually, it combines forces with the Maranon River and together, these two rivers form the headwaters of the Amazon. The confluence begins at Nauta,100 km downstream from Iquitos, Peru, the furthest point inland on the Amazon where the ocean - faring ships travel.

Standing on the riverboat SS Hullaga, in the heart of the Peruvian Amazon, Fred felt he finally had realized his dream. It was the second week of July,1963. But, he wondered if it was real as the birds above chased each other like streaking comets. They were nose- diving for fish under the swift-running current.

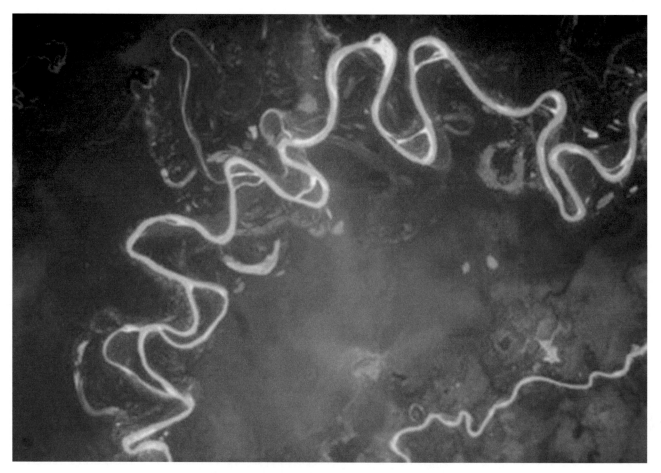

The Meandering Ucayali

The Hullaga reminded Fred of the kind of faded-white old wooden Mississippi paddle wheeler on which he always longed to travel. Staring above into the humid bright sun, in front of his small semi- private cabin on the second deck, he looked down at the hectic scene unraveling on the dockside below.

Local passengers were carefully stepping onto the well-worn wooden gangplanks with their faded red, blue and yellow colored hammocks slung over their backs; mother's carrying infants, fathers carrying young children, some older worried faces carrying bags of fruit, clothing and other possessions.

Pigs were squealing in worn wooden crates that were awkwardly lifted onboard by young, strong-armed mates in flip flops and bathing suits. The next day, we came to know those *porcos* would be part of our nightly dinner.

The muddy Pucallpa riverbank was freshly showered from an early morning rain in this jungle. Today, at noon, we were about to set sail after six days of *"mañana,"* the standard answer from the captain, who grinned through his two gold front teeth. He reminded Fred of Humphrey Bogart.

Everyday, for a week, when Fred had asked him when the boat would leave, always he replied, *"mañana."*

Anxiously, he now watched as many burlap sacks of onions were being loaded onto his boat. The skin trader also brought piles of his ocelot hides onboard. Each day the water- line level of the Hullaga crept closer to the top of the muddy-brown Ucayali, lapping and licking upwards against the groaning, creaking boat.

This isn't Cincinnati, Pittsburgh or Cleveland, Fred reminded himself. He remembered the hobos his Grandma Rose used to feed with her pea soup when six-year-old Freddie and his older brother George lived with her.

Every week she would brew her aromatic delight filled with carrots, small chunks of potatoes, onions and simmering stewing beef. This warmed our souls during the cold New Jersey winter.

Sometimes, she would make an extra large pot and on those days, at lunchtime usually, there would be a knock at the back door. In her thick Polish/Yiddish immigrant accent, Grandma would tell me to open it.

Quickly, little Freddie would let the strangers in from the cold and the two or three leathery, raggedy men in baggy worn pants would shuffle a few steps down into the dank unfinished basement. Quietly, they would sit on the wooden stools by a rickety gray workbench as Grandma Rose carefully brought down her steaming pot of thick pea soup. Fred would get the spoons, soup bowls, and hunks of fresh rye bread.

Then, he sat nearby them on a small stool listening to the men as they slurped with satisfaction. They spoke in a language that sounded like Grandma's accent.

"Where are you going," young Freddie asked them? And they would tell him of their travels on freight cars to far off places from Passaic and the Erie-Lackawanna Railroad station near Grandma's house: Cincinnati, Pittsburgh and Cleveland.

Fred's wanderlust was nourished by Grandma Rose's pea soup.

I couldn't imagine at that time that little Freddie would eventually grow up to become me. Although, at times, I struggled to follow the mold, and the fine life examples and standards set by my parents, I was lured and tugged by the unknown.

This curiosity, in part, is what led me to this first of many expeditions and travels into the Amazon, and South America, now, almost sixty years ago.

Grandma Rose with 6 months Freddie.

"Is this Cabin 6 mate?" a tall, lanky young man with twinkling light blue eyes and auburn curly hair asked.

«Why yes,» I replied.

"I guess we're the only two gringos on this boat. My name is Leo, what's yours mate?"

I introduced myself. We learned we were sharing Cabin 6, no bigger than only a large closet with a bunk bed and a little rusty white sink, with cold water.

I walked into the cabin with Leo to show him about.

"My stuff is on the bottom, but I'll move to the top since I'm shorter," I said.

And Leo had no complaints. I would rather be above him so I wouldn't hear him shifting about.

"It's tight quarters, but better than standing all night," he laughed, putting his large black backpack on the lower bunk.

"Where you heading?" I asked.

"The Orinoco to pan for gold," he answered excitedly. "Quit my dull engineering job back in Melbourne and here I am chasing my dream, and you?"

"And me? I guess I'm here just trying to figure out my life, my future. Getting away from the States for the first time and trying to figure it all out. I'm doing some adventure traveling. I always wanted to see the Amazon."

I didn't feel I knew Leo well enough to tell him my whole story. I just had left George Washington University Law School and had recently signed a high school English teaching contract in Bellows Falls, Vermont, to start at the end of August. But now it was only July 8,1963, and like the poet Robert Frost wrote: "I have miles to go before I sleep."

It had been one Spring cherry-blossomed day during my first year of law school in Washington, D.C.,

and I had arranged to meet with Louis Untermeyer, then the Poet Laureate and Consultant of Poetry at The Library of Congress.

Am I out of my mind? I asked myself, as I walked up the steps to the Capital building to his office. It was only a few weeks before that I had cut my contracts class to see President Kennedy greet the King of Morocco at Union Station. Shortly thereafter, I wrote a poem about this experience in the style of E.E. Cummings and now I was asking Untermeyer's opinion of it. I was amazed he accepted my request to see him.

I entered his office nervously, its sweeping views looked down towards the Washington Monument on the Great Mall. His secretary politely led me into this highly respected poet, anthologist and critic's inner sanctum. He looked very dapper in a blue three-piece pin-striped suit sporting a gentle smile and wire-framed eyeglasses.

Extending a handshake, and a courteous hello, I sat by his desk piled with books and manuscripts. He asked my reason for this meeting. I couldn't believe I was sitting in front of the author of the well-known Anthology of Modern American and British Poetry, which I had studied extensively in Mr. Barras' English class at Montclair Academy. I told him how much I admired his anthology and then told him about my confusion about staying in Law School. He asked me to read my poem to him.

After listening, he smiled genuinely with a sparkle in his eyes and said, "I like it. Shows great enthusiasm and patriotism."

But, also, he advised me to graduate law school and continue writing. Then, he grinned in a fatherly way, politely shook my hand and bid me adieu.

My immediate reaction was more confusion. I didn't want to stay in law school but practically, I knew he was right.

I hadn't performed too well on the Law School Boards. But, evidently, I convinced the admissions interviewer that I really wanted to attend law school. So, they gave me a chance.

Three months later in June, after deciding to leave, I was on my way to Peru to visit my pen pals in Lima to begin my unexpected journey along the Ucayali, 1,500 river miles from Pucallpa to Iquitos, the furthest port inland on the Amazon.

I was looking out of the airplane window, with mixed emotions, as we left Washington. Well, now I had quit law school. I knew I had disappointed my parents, particularly my father who always had high hopes I would enter the family lumber and building business and practice real estate law.

What really contributed to my decision to leave had been my visits to two uncles who both worked for the Federal Government. One was an Assistant Secretary at The Labor Relations Board and the other worked on Tax issues for the IRS. Every time I visited them, they were always looking ashen grey behind a pile of legal briefs. This is definitely not for me, I would think to myself. I don't know what I want but it can't be a life indoors like this.

I did like the study of the law, but not the life-style.

"Looks like we got a full boat - load of passengers," Leo said interrupting my thoughts,

"Looks that way," I agreed. We both stared down at the last of the passengers straggling onboard.

Just then the captain was edging towards us on the narrow passageway by our cabin near the pilot house. Leo and I stepped aside to let him pass by.

"*Cuando vamos*?" I asked in my best of high school/college Spanish.

"*Pronto*!" he grinned through his gold teeth...and walked on.

"Oh yeah, pronto like *manana*," I joked, and then continued to gaze down at the water reflecting about my sojurn to get here.

Shortly after I made my decision to leave law school, I had contacted my former Headmaster and mentor from Montclair Academy, Thomas Hall Jr., to ask for his guidance in what career path I might follow. Kindly, he invited me to his home in South Shaftesbury, Vermont. "Sounds like you need to take a long walk," he said." Come on up to the country, it will do you some good."

Two weeks later, I was in his cozy log home nestled on a hillside looking over the gentle Vermont countryside.

Even though it was now several years since I had graduated from Montclair Academy, it was the rule at school to always address the masters as "Mr." So, I still found it difficult to address my host on an informal first name basis.

Mr. Hall was retired from teaching. He and his wife Betsy offered me a safe-haven from my uncertain future for a few days. After much discussion and pleasant long walks, Mr. Hall, a tall lean man with a wise smile, said, "Fred, I think you should consider teaching.

You were an English major in college and have much to offer your students."

I didn't give it another thought. My mom was a physical education teacher and this might be an interesting pursuit- at least for a while.

When I told Mr. Hall, how I had met Louis Untermeyer just a few months before and read my poem, he stood erect and moving his shoulders back asked, "You know who is my neighbor in that house just below?"

Before I could answer, he said, "Robert Frost."

"Really," I said, with undisguised joy. "He wrote my favorite poem about the two roads diverged in a wood, and I took the one less traveled by, and that has made all the difference."

Later that day, Mr. Hall made some telephone calls to his contacts in the Vermont Department of Education.

"Seems there are a few opportunities for you Fred," he smiled with a sense of accomplishment. "There's an opening for a high school English teacher way up North in St. Albans and a job over in Bellows Falls by the Connecticut River across from New Hampshire. Maybe we can call and get you an interview in the morning."

Within a day, I found my way to the Bellows Falls High School for a job interview with the superintendent of schools and the school's principal.

Bellows Falls High School was an impressive three story stone Gothic structure with the motto engraved above the front entrance: "Enter to Learn, Go Forth To Serve."

Apprehensively, at age 22, I had my first teaching job interview. After a brief exchange of greetings, the superintendent got right to the point peppering me with a few questions: "Where did you go to college? So, you majored in English? Would you mind the cold weather here?"

I answered and told him about my love of writing prose and poetry. And, within ten minutes, Mr. Holland, the Superintendent said, "Congratulations, you're hired."

Later, I was told that they were really hard up for an English teacher, and I was the first interested prospect to come along.

But, I felt proud and grateful to Mr. Hall. I had my first teaching job. It was something to look forward to after I returned from Peru.

"We'll offer you a starting salary of $4,000 and $50 for directing the senior high play and another $50 for being advisor to the yearbook for a total of $4,100. Is that agreeable?"

"Why yes," I gulped, although I really didn't know if it was all right. At least it was something. And besides, I always wanted to spend the four seasons in New England watching the leaves turn colors and experiencing deep snow.

"What are you doing the rest of the summer?" Charlie Davis the principal asked.

I paused for a minute, then replied with a sense of adventure, "Well, sir, I am leaving for Peru to see my pen pal and maybe the Amazon Jungle," I said just to see their reactions.

Their jaws both dropped. "Really, they said, almost in unison, "Will we ever see you again?" Holland asked.

"I hope so. I'll send you a post card on my travels."

"Well, we open school for the teachers on August 27th and school starts just after Labor Day. We hope to see you then. Safe travels," he added with some sense of parental concern.

We shook hands. Now, I was going forth to serve!

But, the sounds of the Hullaga's whistle crashed into my thoughts as the paddle wheel started to churn the brown river water, full steam ahead. The young mates below hurriedly unraveled the heavy worn ropes tying us to the dockside. Finally, we are about to set sail at 4 o'clock in the afternoon with a full-laden boat of cargo and passengers. The boat seemed to rock from side -to -side as we slowly got underway and left the red earth of the Pucallpa riverbanks and into the next phase of my life. Pucallpa, I later learned is a Quechua word for "red earth." Quechua is a mix of Inca and Spanish dialect.

Where will we be tonight? What's next on this great adventure, I wondered as the Hullaga started to slip away from the dock and the paddle wheel of the riverboat began to churn. Everyone started to settle in for the long haul upstream, although as I soon learned, this was a local bus ride for many who were returning home to their neighboring villages with their purchases in Pucallpa. Some now settled into their hammocks or walked about and stood watching the river. Kids scampered about and played tag, while some mothers nursed their babies and a few children some of whom appeared to be 2 years old just drinking from their mother's breasts, like a milk bottle. The mother's tenderly enjoying and caressing their young ones.

"The boat seems to be rocking," said Leo. "Something's not right with the balance. Maybe we have too much weight?"

"You think so?" I asked. I didn't want to believe him, but I was thinking he might be right. After all, the boat was a week late in sailing because the captain kept loading cargo and the water line kept dipping lower and lower. Now, I noticed the swaying of the boat as the captain and head-mate kept turning the boat left and right to avoid the sandbars that suddenly appeared.

Since this was dry season, the water level of the river was 20 sometimes 30 feet lower than rainy season. The sand bars became an obstacle course. A young mate stood on the roof of the riverboat as a lookout to call out when he spotted these sandbars.

As we left port and were about an hour out of town, the sun was lowering into the distant sky. Shadows appeared on the river and I noticed a certain nervousness tremoring among the passengers as the boat continued to rock unsteadily.

Leo and I gazed at the trees on the riverbank as they passed us by. Then, we heard arguing in the pilothouse. I walked quietly near to hear the captain shouting at the skin trader and the potato trader.

"What are they saying?" asked Leo.

Water level at dry season.
by Frederick L. Kramer

"Don't really know," I said. "They are talking in Quechua. That's a dialect of Incan and Spanish the natives all speak here. My friends in Lima told me about this."

But soon, we all knew what had happened. The paddle wheel slowed to almost a halt and the boat started to turn around.

"The captain made a decision to head back to port," the mates were saying in Spanish and Quechua.

There's too much weight on the boat.

And so ended our first big day on the river. Silently, the Hullaga crept back to Pucallpa in the dusk, like a dog with its tail between its legs, humbled. Leo and I watched the boat tie up to the pier. Dinner was being served on the stern, women and children first (rice, beans, tea), and the mates started to unload many sacks of ocelot skins, potatoes and yuca.

"*Cuando vamos*?" I asked the young mate rapidly approaching Leo,"

"*Manana pronto*!" he replied as he scooted past us.

"Well, here goes another *manana*," I told Leo with sarcasm. "You want to bet what time *manana* we leave?"

"I'm gettin' hungry," Leo said, scratching his thin stomach, and you?"

"Me too," I replied and we both walked towards the winding stairway at the stern. As we descended, I noticed the large paddlewheels resting silently and also waiting for *manana*.

Most of the women and children had finished their dinner as the mates were clearing the two long tables covered with red and white checkered oil cloth. Many of the men were standing by eagerly waiting to sit down on the long wooden benches by the tables. This was a family–style affair. Soon we got to meet our fellow travelers, none of whom ever heard of Pittsburgh, Cincinnati or Cleveland.

As the last of the women and children departed, the men sat down quickly like a game of musical chairs. Leo and I sat next to each other near one end of a table. The conversation was lively amongst the locals. I sensed they were all chatting about how the boat turned around because of the overload. Many were probably wondering how long their trip was going to be delayed. I wondered too but I didn't care. This was all a novel experience. But then I thought, will I ever make it back to Bellows Falls?

"You want some rice?" Leo asked. A large bowl of white rice was being passed around.

"Sure." Then, I passed it to my right, I offered the bowl to a little older man with a deeply, wrinkled face.

"*Quiere*? You want?" I spoke in Spanish and English. He giggled and nodded "Si." I wondered if he spoke Spanish or Quechua. I know he didn't speak English.

Tonight, we just had rice, brown beans, tea and home-made white biscuits. What else could you ask for? Our voyage cost only $10 plus ten extra dollars for the semi-private cabin. When I bought the passage I thought it was a real bargain for all this distance.

Everyone chatted among themselves and their friends, but I noticed that, like children, they kept glancing curiously towards Leo and I, the two gringos.

We finished our mini-supper and the few light bulbs on the boat were turned on and darkness descended over the jungle canopy. The problem with having the lights turned on was that they attracted swarms of mosquitoes. So, they were turned off after an hour. Along the outside deck of the boat, the women and children were comfortably swaying in their hammocks that the men had fixed up to the ceiling hooks above. Bedtime was approaching for most. Some of the men lingered at the bow or stern smoking cigarettes. And now the mosquitoes joined the party. Not just one mosquito, two mosquitoes or three but a countless number, a whole world of mosquitoes.

"It's going to be a long night," I sighed.

Leo nodded. Now I understood why the men all seemed to be chain smoking. This was the number one defense against the hordes of mosquitoes buzzing about our ears, eyes and everywhere.

"Want one?" Leo offered.

"Well, I don't really smoke, but I guess it will help," I accepted his offer with mixed emotions.

He offered me a matchbook to light the Camel he gave me, my mind flashed back to my grammar school days when I used to smoke a pack of Pall Malls with my buddy Billy. In those days, any kid could walk into a little candy store, buy a pack of bubble gum with baseball cards, ju ju beads, string licorice red or black, and a pack of cigarettes.

And in those days, in the early fifties, we would walk a mile plus to school through the Third Ward Park by ourselves, unaccompanied by any adult except for maybe an older brother or a friend or two. Sometimes we even walked alone without giving a thought that anyone might harm us.

Billy and I would meet every Wednesday after school and stop in to the local candy store. Billy was bolder than me, so he would walk right up to the counter and ask for a pack of Pall Mall for his mother.

"Anything else," the storeowner would ask, shifting his moustache from side to side.

"Oh yeah," Billy would always say, "and a pack of bubble gum with baseball cards."

He was a wild kid who liked to fight everyone in the schoolyard and even beat me up one time after my 10th birthday party for no reason I ever could figure out. Maybe he was jealous I had a lot of attention and he was an only child. But still we were friends for this one event of smoking, in a little make- shift hut we built together in the woods up the street from my parent's house.

Every Wednesday for a month or two, we would light up and cough ourselves silly. We would talk about school, our parents, maybe a girl or two and just kick back from the stress of our lives with parents, family and school work.

After we smoked maybe a half a pack, we buried the package in a tin cup under some brush in the hut. Then, we would chew bubble gum to disguise our breath, see what baseball cards we got and walk home as if nothing ever happened. This was our little big secret.

"Damn mosquitoes," Leo swore, slapping his face trying to hit a dozen in one swipe.

"It's gettin' a bit late. Think I'll get some sleep, if I can. It's been a long day," he sighed.

"It's gonna' be a longer night I think with all these mosquitoes buzzing around,"

I said while coughing a little from the cigarette smoke I didn't mean to inhale.

"No matter, I'm turnin' in. See you in the mornin' mate." Leo entered the cabin and shut the door.

I snuffed out on the railing the last of the cigarette and tossed the butt into the river, and listened to the silence of the night descend upon the boat.

Children were asleep in the swaying hammocks, cuddled in their mother's arms. Everyone was tuckered out from the events of the day, first finally leaving port and then having to accept the disappointment that we went nowhere. Now, we all eagerly awaited an early start tomorrow before dawn.

I didn't want to go into my cabin. It was only about 10 o'clock and the cabin was stuffy with no fan and only slats in the cabin door for some fresh air. Sounds glorious that we're in the Amazon jungle, but not tonight for this gringo.

So, I walked again to the bow of the second deck in front of the pilot house. Some of the men and young mates had gathered there all smoking cigarettes and occasionally waving hands to fan the mosquitoes away. I smiled and said, *"Hola.* Cigarette *por favor."*

One of the men, smiled and offered me one

"*Gracias*," I said wondering if he spoke Quechua or Spanish. I just listened and became one of the boys.

After about a half hour, they all started to wander back to their hammocks and reluctantly I gave in and went to the cabin.

I could hear Leo snoring. He must be exhausted, but now I have mosquitoes and snoring to contend with. So, I stared into the starry evening sky and thought about my long voyage to get here.

My plane from Washington, D.C., first landed in Bogota, Colombia, for a few hours and then onto Quito, Ecuador. I stopped there for three days to see this city at nearly 10,000 feet altitude known as the highest capital city in the world. A Ecuador means "equator" and this is the midpoint between North and South America, tropical and subtropical.

Arriving in Quito about four in the afternoon, I hopped into a taxi and asked the driver to take me to a small inexpensive hotel. How trusting I was in my youth. The driver joked and said he knew a comfortable rooming house owned by a lady who had three marriages and made enough *dinero* to buy the house.

From the outside, the three -story wooden *casa* looked tidy and clean. I entered and the owner, a very attractive lady checked me in and gave me the room key – number 4 on the second floor. I started to carry my duffle bag up the creaky wooden stairs. About midway up, a man's voice shouted down to me.

"Come on in, the door is open."

A bit surprised and curious, I reached the second floor and peered into the first room on the left.

"Come on in."

As I entered, I saw a thin middle- aged man polishing the butt of a pistol and a rifle by his side.

"Don't worry, I ain't gonna' shoot yah. My name is Bill, what's yours?" he said in a southern accent.

"I'm Fred." Now I wondered if I would ever see Mr. Holland again.

"What brings yah to these here parts?"

"Oh, just traveling to see some friends in Lima, Peru."

"Oh, Lima, been there once." I got a wild orchid farm in Tampa, Florida. Wild Bill's Tropical Orchids." I'm goin' into the Oriente province where the wild orchids grow. Wannah come?

"Well, I don't know. How long you gonna' be there?"

"About a month or so, unless the Aucas or Jivaros get me first."

"The Aucas and Jivaros?" I asked.

"Yeah, they're enemies on opposite sides of the river. The Jivaro use blow guns with poison darts. They like to shrink heads too! The Aucas use poison- tipped spears. But, the orchids are beautiful."

Courtesy of Wikipedia.com

Now I was really happy that I signed that teaching contract in Bellows Falls, Vermont. I had the perfect excuse.

"Sounds like a fantastic experience. Let me go to my room first and will talk later."

"OK," he agreed and off I went to my Room 4 across the hall from Wild Bill who went back to polishing his gun butt.

"Damn mosquitoes," I muttered to myself as I slapped my face.

The whole boat was asleep now, even those *porcos* not knowing their fate.

The moon rose high, shining brightly over and across the swiftly flowing Ucayali.

Feeling like a prisoner, I escorted myself into my tiny cabin 6, opened the creaking narrow door, looked at snoring Leo curled into a fetal position. He seemed like he could sleep through an explosion.

Now closing the door, it was dark inside the cabin. I slipped out of my flip- flops, tried quietly to walk step by step up the rickety wooden ladder and fell exhausted into my bed.

Just as I lapsed into deep sleep, I was awakened by an annoying buzzing in my ear, which would be the first of many through this first night onboard and throughout the 1,600 mile voyage.

Trying to fall back to sleep for the third time, I couldn't wait for dawn to arrive so the mosquitoes would leave us alone during the heat of the day. However, Leo didn't seem to mind since he never stirred.

I remembered how I got here.

Wild Bill had said, "If you can't make it into the Oriente with me, I'll tell you about a great trip you should take up the Ucayali from Pucallpa. You can fly in from Lima over the Andes. You'll get off in Iquitos. By the way, you can buy a lot of semi-precious gemstones there; aqua marine, tourmalines, topaz… you might even make a few bucks when you get back to the States."

The sudden noise of the paddlewheel engines starting up woke me. Is it morning already? I noticed a feint light appearing through the cabin door slats.

I realized we're going to head upstream now. My mind wanted to hop down the ladder to see us take off. But, my body was slow to move. I slept naked, can't stand clothes on me when I sleep. I reached for my shorts and started down the ladder in bare feet. No movement from Leo. I opened the cabin door and still it was a little dark outside, but the approaching dawn gave some shadowy light. Two mates were on the dock unraveling the ropes tying the Hullaga to its evening berth. I could smell the captain's cigarette flowing from the pilot house. He wasn't wasting anytime to leave port.

Below, I could see many lingering in their hammocks although they were standing along the handrails watching the action. A few were already smoking. Some sleepyhead kids were standing by, rubbing their tired eyes. In my enthusiasm I wanted to wake up Leo. But, what the heck, I thought let him sleep.

The ropes were untied and the Hullaga abruptly backed away from the pier. Pucallpa was asleep. There was no official send - off, no waving hands like yesterday when it seemed half the town was there watching us depart. It was the major event of the day for the locals sending upstream their relatives, loved ones, friends and two gringos off to their villages.

With puffs of diesel rising into the air, the boat stopped its backward motion and began to thrust forward with paddlewheels turning. Again, we were on our way. The thrill of the unknown lay ahead.

"What's up mate. We on our way?" Leo yawned, scratching his uncombed hair and nearly banging his head on the cabin door.

"Morning mate. Have a good sleep? Mosquitoes didn't bother you, did they?"

"Reckon not, I was bushed. Here comes the sun," he said as the new day began leaving Pucallpa behind.

We took turns splashing cold water on our faces in the lonely sink and brushing our teeth. The cabins came with two small hand towels to dry ourselves.

The river was quiet except for the thrashing of the paddlewheel throwing the foaming water up into the paddles. It was mesmerizing to watch this constant motion in the stern. Two bathrooms were located there and were well-used, particularly at this time of the day.

Clang, clang, clang, rang the bell on the ceiling next to the small kitchen. It was 7:30 am and first call for breakfast, women and children first. All we were served was hot tea and biscuits. No wonder the 2- year- old kids wanted their mother's milk.

Before you knew it, there was the clang, clang, clang again. The second call to breakfast. Leo and I joined the men and that same gentle small old man sat next to me again. We nodded hello.

He grinned and poured some hot tea. Then he passed the teapot on to me.

On the table near us was a plate full of biscuits. Everyone respectfully selected one and continued with early morning chatter.

"Going to be a long day on the river mate," Leo turned to me and said.

"Reckon so. Iquitos is a long way from here, too."

After breakfast, people found a quiet spot for themselves as the hum of the paddlewheel churning took over the silence on the river. Occasionally birds flocked by, a few diving into the water to catch breakfast.

Once in a while, someone in a canoe glided by the boat going somewhere. And the trees and many shades of green jungle kept passing us, as the sun crept higher into the mid - morning sky. Rising with it, was the heat of the day and the shady side of the boat became the place to be.

The constant breeze from the movement of the boat was refreshing. The captain seemed happy now, as he was talking non- stop in the pilot house to his head-mate. And just as all seemed in order, the young mate on the roof shouted to the captain who immediately blew the boat whistle. The paddlewheel instantly shut down and the Hullaga once again was forced to slow to an unwanted halt.

"Must be a sandbar," I yelled to Leo who was writing in his diary while lying on his bed in the cabin. He shut his book and stood up carefully, leaving the cabin cautiously, not to hit his head again.

Then, something amazing happened. I thought it was ingenious. Our captain isn't so crazy after all. To get the Hullaga safely through the sandbar which was protruding halfway into the middle of the river, and with the water too shallow on the far side, he turned the boat around. By dropping anchor, he was able to stabilize the Hullaga at a standstill, while the paddlewheels kept turning at a constant medium- fast pace. Thus, the whitewash of the foaming water churning from the paddlewheel cut a pass through the sandbar.

This took about an hour. When the paddlewheel finally slowed down, the captain had the anchor lifted. Everyone fell silent. All aboard looked straight ahead and the Hullaga inched forward like a snake creeping quietly before it struck for the kill.

No one inside the pilot house was talking. The captain had the wheel. The mate on top of the boat was shouting out *"Derecho* =right. Izquierda= left." Some women crossed themselves, praying that the boat wouldn't capsize.

Finally, we were free from the grip of the sandbar. The bow broke into the clear pathway. All seemed to breathe a sigh of relief. The horn sounded twice,

it was a message from the captain we were okay. People smiled, some clapped their hands in approval while others cheered. Little did we know this would be the first of many such moments for the next 1,500 miles.

The morning wore on uneventfully except for a sudden awful blood curling squeal coming from the kitchen below. I climbed down the circular flag- pole stairs landing near the kitchen. The chef had just slit the throat of one of the *porcos.* What a morning. I decided to go look at the paddlewheel, to think about something else.

But for the first few minutes, all I could think about was that poor little pig soon to be our dinner. The chef was probably thinking how much work he'd have to do to clean the carcass and prepare the meal.

The bubbling water flying off the paddlewheel turned my mind to a different direction. I thought upon my first day's arrival into Pucallpa and Wild Bill's enthusiastic suggestion that led me here.

I recalled that my flight left Lima about 8:30 am on a DC-3. We flew above the clouds, higher than 15,000 - feet over the Andes. The cabin wasn't pressurized. We had to breathe through our oxygen masks. Looking out the window, I saw - not too far below - these angular, barren, rocky - crested and sometimes snow covered mountains grown together for endless miles. We definitely don't want to crash here, I thought.

After almost an hour over this rugged terrain, the landscape instantly changed. The mountains vanished. Ahead lay the Amazon canopy. It looked as if there was nothing but broccoli tops of trees below. The whole world was now green.

Clang, clang, clang, the boat's lunch bell rang, interrupting my thoughts.

After lunch, of the usual rice, brown beans, biscuits and tea, I took a nap. The heat of the day was upon us, but the movement of the boat filtered a warm breeze through the door slats. Leo stood outside smoking and I decided to take a siesta, drifting away into the hum of the paddlewheel turning round n' round, n' round….

I dreamed about the DC 3 as it lowered itself into the jungle below. I wondered where we would land, since I didn't see any signs of civilization nor of any airport.

Now, I saw the winding brown river- the Ucayali. We hovered a few hundred feet above the tree- tops and dropped quickly onto a field with a soccer goal post at one end coming to a bumpy halt. The plane spun around and headed for the tree line on the far side of the field and came to an abrupt halt by a large mango tree filled with fruit like huge green gum drops. There were some wooden benches under the tree. This was the Pucallpa airport.

The stewardess opened the latch to the exit door and the humid air rushed in. Cautiously, I stepped down from the plane's skimpy stairway onto the uneven ground. A young boy ran towards me yelping like a puppy, "*Senor, senor*; Mister, Mister,"

He tugged at my backpack. I sensed he didn't want to rob me, but help me.

We stood together, my new amigo and I, waiting for the rest of the luggage to be tossed onto the ground. I walked over to my bag knowing it was too big for my young friend to carry. But he insisted on dragging the duffle bag, too. So, I chuckled a little and marveled at how eager he was to help me, and make some money.

My new *amigo* started towards a waiting old car with my bags. I assumed this was the taxi. A middle-aged man, the driver with a pencil thin black moustache, got out of the car and promptly asked, "*Donde, donde*?"

I responded, "hotel, hotel," assuming it was the same word in Spanish. My new puppy hopped in the front of the car, I sat in the back, and off we went to the hotel. How trusting I was.

"*Que es su nombre*?" I asked the puppy.

"Vitor Raul, Vitor Raul,"

Landing in Pucallpa
by Frederick L. Kramer

CHAPTER 2

VITOR RAUL The Lagoon
at YARINACOCHINA

Some years later, thinking about this first expedition of mine outside the security from all I had known in the U.S., it is both amusing and scary and surprising to consider just how naïve, innocent, impetuous and intuitively trusting we are in our youth.

My entry into the Amazon had no planning or prior thought except for that chance meeting with Wild Bill in Quito, Ecuador. And, in reality, if it were not for another chance meeting in San

Francisco, a few years earlier, when I was investigating the possibility of attending Law School, I might never have had these unique experiences.

Regarding my travels into remote places, I never considered the possibilities of any physical danger, through mishap or diseases like malaria, yellow fever, dengue, polio, or unfriendly animals: snakes, piranhas, jaguars, caimans, or untrustworthy humans.

In hindsight, this was a miscalculation. At times, there were challenges to my trusting nature, but still an unyielding belief that everything would work out OK.

Somewhere, I did have a guardian angel that protected me. And in this case, one of my guardian angels were the Zamora's.

During the summer of my Junior year in college, I had travelled to San Francisco for interviews at Stanford and the new Hastings College of Law. On the second day there, I took a Grey Line sightseeing bus. Sitting across from me was a very pleasant couple who smiled at me and I said hello to them. The *senora*, Mrs. Zamora, spoke English, but her husband Arturo only understood Spanish. Yet, we very much managed to enjoy our conversation in English and my high school/college Spanish. I learned they were from Lima, Peru, and in the U.S. for the first time. After the city tour, we exchanged addresses. Little did I know then, that the Zamora's would become my home base in a distant land in the not too distant future.

When I had made the decision to leave Law School, I felt the need to venture outside of the continental United States and expose myself to a totally different culture. I considered going to Europe, but that seemed to me like going to museums and churches. The appeal of using my Spanish language skills and travelling to South America was stronger. So, I wrote the Zamora's, and they invited me to visit them. For how long, I had no idea. And to see what else, I had no idea … until I met up with Wild Bill in Quito, Ecuador.

I thought about the ride from the rural airport into the frontier town of Pucallpa. It took about a half hour on a tree shaded, winding, bumpy dirt road, over watery pot holes still wet from an earlier jungle rain.

Thick tangles of vines crowded a variety of dense trees. All this timber reminded me of my father's lumber yard where I used to work after school in June for a month, before going away to summer camp in New Hampshire.

I remembered the fresh woody smell of Carolina and Georgia pine when we unloaded the boxcars at the rail siding in the lumberyard. My dad and I used to leave the house about 7:00 am. Work started at 8:00. Everyone punched in to the office time clock. Since I was the boss's son, my dad wanted me to be there early.

Because I was the smallest worker at ages 14, 15, and 16, I would be hoisted up by two of the bigger workmen and climb up to the top of the woodpile of neatly stacked 1x6, 1x8, 1x10, 1x12's, sometimes 8, 12, 16 - feet long. Other boxcars had 2 x 4's and the most difficult to handle were boxcars of Anderson Windows. The three-paneled bowed bay windows were the heaviest to move.

Normally, there was only about four-feet of headroom, and it would be hot and stuffy in the boxcar. So, as fast as I could, I would start to pick and shovel out the boards of cut timber to the outstretched waiting arms and hands of the workmen standing on the truck. We wore gloves so as not to get any skin piercing splinters, but sometimes it might happen.

The quicker I accomplished this unloading process, the faster I could get some extra headroom and, eventually, be able to stand up straight. The fresh pine smell was delightful and I pretended I was in a forest to take my mind away from the laborious task. Couldn't wait till we had a coffee break at 9:15.

But this scene gradually changed, as my taxi came into a clearing. The town of Pucallpa lay ahead. It was not yet the dangerous place it would become fifty years later as a clandestine growing field for cocoa production and underground anti-government terrorist groups. Back then, it was a laid - back, rural jungle town hidden in the interior.

I no longer felt like I was back home, in the lumberyard, but in another world far away, knowing no one except for my new amigo, Vitor Raul.

The main street was dirt and lined with wood- framed buildings. Ramshackle concrete structures, some with glassless window openings with no protection and others with iron grills and shutters to prevent intruders. It reminded me of the kind of Wild West town I had seen in the Western movies.

The hotel was a concrete structure, a very basic building, no frills, but it was in the center of the town. The walk down to the boat landing was only a couple of hundred yards. My young puppy Vitor had helped me to my room with my bags. He was my new friend and evidently, guardian. He asked if I was hungry and took me to a restaurant on the main street where I bought us lunch.

The restaurant was small, crowded and noisy, but the aroma of rice, beans, fried plantains and roast pork was delicious.

We sat by an open window - shaped aperture where we could watch the activity on the street. This Pucallpa was alive with a kind of lazy energy. No one was ever in a rush to go anywhere, yet there seemed to be a certain enthusiasm for living that was refreshing to me. Houseflies danced on our table as the meal was served. Not even the whirling ceiling fan could keep them away from our food. But it tasted good anyway.

After lunch we walked down to the boat landing to see when the next paddlewheel was going upstream to Iquitos. There, we saw the Hullaga and the captain, a Humphrey Bogart look-a-like, standing on the bow and that's where I encountered our first, *manana*.

I paid the captain for my cabin. When I asked him what time *manana* we would leave, he shrugged his shoulders and said, "*posible en la tarde*;" Maybe in the afternoon. His two gold front teeth glimmered in the afternoon sunlight. After two days of this standard answer, Vitor Raul offered to show me the Lagoon at Yarinacochina.

The next morning, my third day in Pucallpa, about eight – thirty, Vitor Raul walked into the same *restaurante* where I was having breakfast: omelet, toast, orange juice *y* café.

"Mister Federico, Buenas dias. Hoy vamos para Yarinachina," he said filled with enthusiasm

Already, he knew my routine. First, he had gone to the hotel and learned I was having breakfast down the street.

When I asked him to sit down and tell me about the possibility of the Hullaga leaving today, he laughed. He told me the boat wouldn't leave for two more days. Earlier, he said he had spoken with the captain and assured me this was so. Vitor said the captain is too busy making money by having more and more cargo loaded onto the boat.

I offered Vitor a breakfast, which he gladly accepted. As we talked further about our proposed adventure for today, I realized that my new friend had the day already planned for me. His cousin, who owned the taxi, would pick us up at ten o'clock and he said we will go to this beautiful Laguna Yarinacohcina outside of town.

I asked Vitor Raul about his family. He said his father had died when he was young. He lived with his *madre* and younger brother and sister. He went to school when he could, but would rather be in the big world and with the nature. He tried to earn money for his family by going to the airport everyday. There, he helped passengers with their baggage and takes them to his cousin's taxi.

I began to feel like his older brother, someone he could confide in and talk to about life. But, he also became my teacher, because soon I would learn about the local environment through his inquisitive eyes.

After breakfast, as we walked back to the hotel, I asked him why he wasn't in school today. A little embarrassed, he admitted he would rather be my tour guide and show me Yarinachochina.

We waited outside the hotel for his cousin as the heat of the day crept into the late morning air. We watched the people amble up and down the street. Some women were holding an umbrella to shade themselves from the hot rising sun.

A few moments later, Vitor's cousin announced his arrival with a double beep, beep, from the horn. Quickly, we hopped in and drove out of town.

We were driving back towards the airport. But shortly, the road split and we took the turn to the right, which became a bumpy, dirt pathway barely wide enough for two cars. Vitor Raul and his cousin were chattering away while I stared through my open car window into the dense thicket of forest. This time, I didn't see two – by - fours from my dad's lumberyard, only green jungle foliage as we entered deeper into the forest.

And then, like magic, after about a half an hour of twisting and turning, we came to a clearing ahead where we could see the water's edge.

Like a curtain opening in a theatre, a whole new scene unfolded.

The taxi came to an abrupt stop in a small clearing off the side of the road. There was a simple rustic hut on stilts. A long canoe lay underneath. Vitor Raul, his cousin and I, lifted the canoe and slipped it into the still water's edge. There was silence all around except for the birds chirping both in the trees and flying about here and there.

I sat in the bow of the canoe, the cousin in the stern and there was a third seat in the middle of this long canoe where Vitor Raul sat. We all paddled in a kind of uniformed, slow rhythm, two or three strokes, then let the canoe glide for a moment just long enough to observe and feel the tranquility surrounding us.

All human speech stopped. The nature was now talking. We had arrived at an inner peace, far away from our personal thoughts and concerns. No wonder Vitor Raul would rather be here than in school, and his cousin would rather be here than in the taxi waiting for a fare at the airport. And I, I was thankful that I left law school though still wondering if I had made a huge career mistake. But, it was too late. The decision was made and here I am, far, far away from all my family expectations.

The finality of realizing now, at this moment, that I had arrived at my new beginning, a new life, just started to sink into my soul. Was I running away from myself? Or, am I now, finally discovering, my true inner nature which has been hidden from me by all the schooling, and societal, cultural demands and those of my family heritage?

The spirits of Yarinacochina were penetrating my veins and offering me a new vision for a new me. What would it be? And little Vitor Raul and his cousin, the taxi man, were my innocent guides into this young tomorrow.

And why am I having this inner debate, when my school chum Steven, (and Junior year college roommate), has known since he was thirteen, that he would be a Dentist? And I'm here, in the middle of nowhere, searching for me?

The lagoon seemed endless, as endless as my inner search. For an hour, we kept up the same rhythm of silence and two or three paddle strokes, and then a long glide. I got the idea that Vitor Raul and his cousin took this canoe ride often, and loved every moment of escaping their every day reality, as I now was too.

The water was calm, the birds chirped overhead and flew in different formations. The heat of the day was shaded by the tree-line as we stayed the course, about thirty feet from the shore-line.

"Quiere comer? Quiere beber?" Vitor Raul asked me.

Breaking the silence of our meditations, I did say, I was getting a little hungry and thirsty. I noticed up ahead, in the far distance, there was a little village. Eventually, we stopped and sat outside a small *restaurante* on a tattered wooden deck where I could take a long view of this peaceful quietude.

Restaurante en Yarinacochina
Courtesy of Wikipedia.com

We sipped our cold sodas of coca cola and stared out to the nature before us. For this one frozen moment, there was no past anymore, only the present. And the new future was revealing itself every moment by moment by moment.

The smell of frying fish wafted through the hot air gently fanned by a slight breeze moving across the lake. We were shaded from the midday sun by the thatched roof over our heads. Every once in a while, Vitor Raul would point to a large bird flying overhead.

Looking into the jungle around us, I hardly could see any light, deep within, as the tangle of vines and leafage was abundant with a variety of vivid lush greenery. Chirping sounds abounded all around announcing the activity of the jungle talking to itself.

"*Comida aqui*," stated Vitor Raul as the fried fish arrived at our table served with white rice, brown beans and fried bananas. It tasted crispy delicious.

Hungrily, we ate and didn't do much talking. Except every once in a while Vitor Raul would ask if I liked the food.

"*Por su puesto*," "of course, of course,"

Happily, I responded and by licking my fingers and smacking my lips. I showed him my approval.

After lunch, we all closed our eyes for a few moments and took a lazy baby nap. I never had felt so still. All the movements in my life had come to a halt. If I could freeze in time, I would choose to remain in this very spot, here on this Earth. No need to move onto Vermont to teach school. But before too soon, we slowly stirred from our quick rest and began our return.

The paddle back to our point of origin was a little tiring. Fortunately, there were three of us to keep the pace moving. But, we all seemed to like the steady rhythm of the three paddle strokes and then a long glide for a 3 or 4 seconds rest. None of us really wanted to leave this sanctuary. But onward we proceeded until the house and the cousin's taxi were in sight.

I began to wonder if the Hullaga had sailed without me. If it did, would I ever get back to Vermont on time to teach school? But, I trusted Vitor Raul.

When we arrived back in town, the cousin drove the taxi down to the dockside to see if the Hullaga was still there. And it was, just sitting there like a rock all alone and only a young mate on board. Vitor Raul did speak with him. He said the captain wasn't onboard, and that the boat wasn't leaving *manana* but probably the next day.

So, I sighed with relief, and realized this was the Jungle time schedule. But anxiously, I was eager to depart for Iquitos. Yet, I was enjoying my extended stay here in Pucallpa, and particularly, my day today in Yarinacochina. But, Leo's shout stirred me from my *siesta*. "Another sand bar mate."

I felt us slowing to a grinding halt. So,

I climbed down from my bed and joined Leo outside the cabin.

Together, we watched as the Hullaga, maliciously churned the foaming water. The captain held the boat steady like a racehorse waiting to run wild. When he was satisfied we had cut a deep enough passageway, he turned the boat around and crept through pass everyone cheered again.

At dusk, the captain parked the boat alongside the steep riverbank. It was too dangerous to travel at night on the river because no one could see the approaching sandbars.

This was our first night upstream from Pucallpa. And tonite dinner was being served with a few pieces of that *porco*, I had heard squealing before.

After the men had finished their dinner, the young mates shouted something in either Quechua or Spanish. People immediately started to follow them off the boat. We were going to walk on a narrow jungle path to a nearby little village for a change of scenery and to get our land legs back.

So, off the boat Leo and I went, into the quickly darkening night.

There were three mates who walked with us. The one in front leading us had a machete and kept hacking at the tall grasses and other vegetation creeping onto the narrow, well-worn foot path, only wide enough for one person, or maybe an adult with a child. There must have been about thirty or forty of us who made this hike into the unknown. Everyone walked alertly, stepped lightly, looking about listening and searching for any signs of a lurking snake.

I don't know about anyone else, but I felt a little scared. Real danger lay in wait. Not like the calm nature hikes when I was a kid at summer camp in lovely New Hampshire searching for salamanders and looking at the ferns. Occasionally, there might be some harmless garden snakes, and maybe a rattlesnake or water moccasin, but here, deep in the jungle thicket, there was fiercer prey.

After a half –hour, we arrived in a clearing where many thatched -roof small houses were scattered about. In the open dirt field, kids were kicking a soccer ball around, even though it was dark. There was no electricity. Only candles illuminated the homes. We followed the mates into a large house that was also a little bar. Everyone was looking at Leo because he was so tall, about 6'3".

At the bar, one of the mates asked me, *"Quiere* ChuChuhuasi*, senor*?"

"ChuChuhuasi?" I asked, *"Que esta?"*

"Muy especial. Es forte!"

"Very special. He said it is strong," I told Leo.

"Let's try it mate," Leo said.

Two shot glasses filled with liquor, like white rum soon arrived. Leo and I clinked our glasses and cautiously sipped a little, wondering if this was our last moment on earth. Who knew what this drink would do to us?

It was smooth, but very strong. The alcohol shot into our heads.

"Strong medicine, eh Leo?"

He nodded in agreement, and asked for one more. The bartender smiled, approvingly.

I didn't want to appear like a "chicken," so I ordered one more, too. But, I winced and smacked my lips as I slowly sipped the drink down. It took a lot of effort for me to finish the second shot.

Later, we learned that the locals make this drink from the distilled bark of the chuchuhuasi tree and let it steep in a mixture of sugar cane alcohol. They claim it is an aphrodisiac. In other parts of the Amazon, chuchuhuasi is used medicinally for ailments like chronic diseases of the nervous system such as Parkinson's, MS and arthritis. It is strong medicine.

But for Leo and I, we just staggered out of the bar and felt no pain when it was time to return to the boat. We were two happy gringos, laughing and stumbling our way through the forest, too numb from the chuchuhasi to be frightened about what might be watching us along the pathway back to the river.

Everyone walked silently and quickly too, trying to keep pace with our guides who seemed to have searchlights for eyes as we walked through the darkness. The men carried their sleepy children. All of us were anxious to get home to our hammocks and tiny cabin.

The only challenge left was to slip, slide down the steep dry, then, muddy riverbank to the gangplank heading onto the boat. Leo and I laughed like two drunken sailors as we entered our little cabin. He flopped onto his thin mattress and I scampered up the ladder and giggled into my pillow.

We both fell asleep. And I dreamt of my afternoon at *La Laguna Yarincochina* with Vitor Raul, only a few days before.

1//14//2015

I had an unexpected revelation. It was after dinner when we took another jungle path and walked into the village of Progresso that I know now I found myself challenged by a life-changing decision

After about a half-mile trek from the Hullaga, at dusk we entered into another little village where I saw many people gathered in the center, standing below a tall pole, about 15 feet, with a single light bulb strung atop of it. They were all listening to a crackling radio excitedly announcing a high school basketball game from a town far away.

This village was called Progresso, because of this one light bulb. There were millions of mosquitoes. The crowd would talk, listen and wave their hands in constant motion trying to fan the mosquitoes away from their eyes…

Such is the life in this paradise.

Leo and I followed our shipmates into a thatched roof bar. Working behind the bar was a young boy, about eighteen-years – old. Also, there was a very pretty girl with olive skin of about the same age. She had long black hair with black thunderbolts for eyes. When she looked at me, I felt a jolt of electric energy that penetrated my heart and soul.

I smiled and not knowing what to say just stumbled with the simple awkward question, *"Como esta?"*

She shyly giggled *"Bien."* But then quickly the young lad stepped in asking *"Que quiere?"*

Leo blurted, "Dos chuchuhuasi." And the young boy grinned as if he knew what was going on between me and the girl.

He brought the drinks. Leo and I clinked glasses remembering we were in for another chuchuhuasi experience.

I asked the young boy his name and he said, Roberto." He introduced his older sister, Rosita. But, just then, his father stepped through the curtain dividing the kitchen from the bar and Roberto went back to work. The father's entrance added a certain perspective to the situation. Could I see myself in his family?

The father asked Roberto a few brief questions and then returned to the kitchen.

Roberto asked me where I was from and where I was going. When I told him I was from New Jersey, he shrugged his shoulders and didn't know what that meant. He had no idea where that was, only to ask, *"Esta en los estados?*

I said *"si,"* and that I was going to Iquitos. Then,I was surprised when he said to me he wished he could go with me and leave what I thought was this paradise- Progresso. He wanted to find a different future- a young tomorrow!

All the while I was talking with Roberto, I kept glancing towards Rosita. At times I felt her gaze at me. What was she thinking? What would life be like if me the gringo was to live with her in this little village? Was this worth trading places for the life in front of me in Vermont? I wondered if I could do it.

Could I just get off the boat, leave everyone I knew my whole life and stay here in Progresso? Would I be welcomed here- *the lone gringo*?

What is my destiny?

I could see the two roads, but what path to take?

1/21/2015

I knew I was enticed by the thrill of a totally different life experience- living in this remote village of Progresso with Rosita.

On the other hand, it seemed like a self-indulgent fantasy. Some kind of absurd craziness stirred up by Grandma Rose's pea soup.

Or was I totally under the influence of the Robert Frost poem, a path less traveled by and that has made all the difference? Was I really smitten by Rosita or just the thought of travelling down an unfamiliar alley to see what might occur?

How could I make a living? Could I teach English here? And who knows if Rosita really would want to be with me. Does she feel the same way?…Yet every time she looked at me, I felt more and more enchanted with the idea. Could I ever become part of her family? Would her father approve of her gringo selection? All I knew was my curiosity grew deeper into her world as I fell deeper into the dream.

Si, it would be interesting and different to live here in Progresso, this one lightbulb village. But did that really make any sense? How would my parents react? And what about the teaching job in Vermont? And then there was my allegiance to Mr Hall for helping me to get the job in Bellows Falls. Bellows Falls - a world away now.

The chuchuhuasi must be getting to me. Leo nudged my arm with his elbow and asked, "Want one more mate?"

I realize now, writing this, the whole idea seemed ridiculous, but I was young enough and carefree enough to take it seriously.

That evening ended abruptly, when Rosita suddenly left the bar and disappeared through the curtain into the kitchen. It was time for us to leave too.

I was happy we found our way safely back to the boat after the second chuchuhuasi. Our small little cabin seemed like a comfortable womb for my dizzying thoughts as I dreamt all night about Rosita and a life in Progresso.

As the sun rose the next morning, and I began to sober up, all thoughts of a life with Rosita in Progresso, slowly slipped into the distance as the paddlewheel of the Hullaga started to churn our way northward towards Iquitos.

CHAPTER 3

IQUITOS

The days dragged on…hot and humid, jungle trees, occasional stops at small landings to let passengers disembark and bring new one's aboard. The Hullaga was a local bus on the Ucayali river highway.

by Frederick L. Kramer

And of course, there were the occasional sandbar drills of

turning the boat around to cut a deeper channel so the boat could pass through.

The slow pace added time to our scheduled arrival in Iquitos, so we were now about a week later than expected. But this gave Leo and me a chance to get to know each other better.

We would talk about his childhood in Australia, and mine in New Jersey. Leo was about 10 years older than me so it felt like he was kind of my older brother.

He elaborated further about his professional life as a civil engineer in Melbourne and how boring it was to sit inside an office and deal with statistical data. He dreamed of the freedom of living in the backcountry of the Amazon and panning for gold. This was his quest and now he was living the dream. He was heading up to the Orinoco River after stopping in Iquitos.

When I told him about my meeting Wild Bill in Quito, Ecuador, and his advice about buying semi-precious gemstones in Iquitos, Leo was enthusiastic and intrigued. The thought of some extra cash appealed to him, so together we plotted our great business venture.

We promised each other that when we reached Iquitos we would pool our money- about $400 each —look for gemstone dealers and purchase some stones. Neither of us had any experience with this commodity, but we thought we could act as though we knew what we were doing.

So now we had a mission in Iquitos.

My other mission was to hop on a plane and fly to Trujillo, Peru and meet my dear friends the Zamora's, who I hoped might still be waiting for me. When I left Lima, we had planned to meet about the 10th of August, but now that the Hullaga is about a week late, I didn't know what to expect. And then there was my contract in Bellows Falls, it seemed so far away now but I couldn't be late for the first day of school.

Reality was starting to set in…

Assignment –February 25, 2015

As the voyage crept forward, the same meals of tea and biscuits for breakfast, rice, beans and biscuits for lunch, and rice, beans with a few little pieces of pork for dinner… insufficient nutrients for my body. I was losing weight and my gums were starting to bleed from the lack of vitamin C. There were no greens except for an occasional salad of lettuce at lunchtime.

One evening when we had walked into another village, I talked with some of the people who came up to Leo and I to see some real live gringos.

One man was a farmer. In a combination of street Spanish and sign language, I told him my gums were bleeding. He asked me to follow him and I told Leo I was going with this man into the unknown to help me with my bleeding gums.

"Buenas suerte," he said, "Good luck."

Together, my newly trusted amigo and I started to walk out of the village into the darkness, lit only by a full moon and into a field of sugarcane. Stars twinkled overhead as the man took out his machete and cut a long stalk of sugarcane.

How wonderful, I thought, humanity is…sometimes. Here, I just met this man and the next thing you know he is helping me with a local remedy for bleeding gums.

He swiftly cut the sugarcane into small pieces. Then, he showed me how to chew it so the fiber would massage my gums and said the sugar would be a good nutrient.

He cut some more stalks into little 4-inch pieces and I put them in my shorts pockets to take with me on the Hullaga. I remember this to this day, some sixty years later.

Gratefully, I told him, *Muchas gracias, gracias.*"

I didn't know if this remedy would work, but it tasted delicious and its rich liquid of pure sugar gave me new energy to carry on.

For a long moment, the two of us stared together into the heavens above. We saw a very bright star-like light, but it was moving.

I said, someday the United States is going to put a man on the moon. He looked at me in disbelief like I was crazy. It was unimaginable to him.

I realized then how innocent everyone was here in the jungle in the middle of nowhere, but somewhere to them. They knew a lot about herbs, plant remedies, but, modern science was beyond them …and me too for that matter. But here the two of us stood in awe, feeling insignificant between the sugarcane fields and outer space.

All time seemed to stop. My life was frozen at this flickering moment, light years away from my past and future.

I was glad when Leo and I finally found our way back to the boat where I once again crawled into my topside bunk, my safe little comfortable womb.

I reflected once again about a life in Progresso, which would never be, Rosita, the stars, my future and, some day maybe soon, the possibility of a man on the moon.

Assignment 3/3/2015

At last, we were approaching somewhat nearer to Iquitos, arriving *manana* at Nauta, where the Maranon meets the Ucayali and together they form the headwaters of the all-mighty Amazon.

All hands were on deck the next day to see this great sight of these two wide watery highways appearing like a chicken wishing bone.

The rivers were fast moving and the muddy brown Amazon appeared ahead like a giant Anaconda.

Everyone gazed in awe. There was a certain smell of excitement and relief as Iquitos was now only about two or three days away.

Leo and I continued our talks, but now, much of the conversation turned towards his preparations for panning for gold. He was making lists he would need to purchase in Iquitos.

And, we fantasized about the fortune we would make with the possible purchase of gem stones.

Finally, our arrival day in Iquitos, which lay in the Amazon Basin along the Amazon, Nanay and Itaya rivers. Its name in the Iquitos language means "the people." The town was originally inhabited by the Napeanos and Iquito people but developed by Jesuit missionaries along the Nanay river about 1757 with the name San Pablo de Napeanos.

By the 1880's, the rubber boom started.

The waterfront district was lined with all sizes of ships carrying cargo and passengers. Even a few large freighters taking cargo from the interior to Europe or the States and also bringing goods from their home ports to Iquitos. Then, smaller boats like the Hullaga would take delivery of some of these items and ferry them back into the interior. Everyone was busy, like worker ants in a big colony.

For me, it was a somewhat sad day. The Hullaga was my home, my security blanket of reflection, at times comfort and discomfort. And now, I was departing reluctantly yet voluntarily…. I had no choice. My return journey to the States, like a boomerang, was about to begin.

But, there were first things first. The line to get off the boat was long. Leo and I watched sentimentally from our deck as the passengers disembarked with their hammocks and bags of stuff and then quickly disappeared into the busy crowd.

The captain started to walk past us.

I wanted to shake his hand and thank him for his expertise. Remember, at first back in Pucallpa I was cursing him because it was always *manana* before we left. But now, he gained my deepest respect. He did know the river Ucayali and he knew the capacity and capability of his boat. So, hats off to him. I just said *"Gracias"* and he smiled walking by. But that smile of his spoke volumes; he knew we hadn't thought much of him in the early days of the journey but we had come to respect his mastery of the river and his boat.

So, what had I learned about myself on this journey so far?

One thing I knew now was to be cautious in my judging of other people.

Have patience and try to curb my fears and anxieties about the unknown.

Not to give into my fantasy about Rosita, and that I couldn't live forever in a place where one cannot imagine about a man on the moon and live in a town with a single light bulb for more than a couple hours, and of course, can't drink too much of that chuchuhuasi which Wild Bill had warned me about.

And that the romantic picture that I had about adventure was not necessarily the reality and it took me many years later to accept that it never is.

There were so many sights and sounds, new foods and fruits, so many different colors, the smiles of innocence- the curiosity of meeting new friends. Of course, who could ever forget the tranquility with Victor Raul at Yarinacochina. And so on and on and on- there would be a lifetime of memories.

Finally, it was our moment to leave. Leo and I were the last passengers off the Hullaga. We shook hands with the mates and tipped them some money. They smiled and laughed with us like family, our brothers, our protectors. And now, we separated like mist over the ocean fog.

Courtesy of Wikipedia.com

Walking down the gangplank of the Hullaga for the last time was a scary feeling filled with separation anxiety. Now we were back into the hustle and bustle of a new moment. Like a horse snorting the air filled with energy, we saw a few dusty taxis waiting nearby.

Leo and I asked a taxi man, who looked like he had just woken up from a nap, to take us to a clean but cheap hotel. Soon we were there in the late morning heat. We checked into our room, put our stuff down and both fell asleep for a while on a real bed. Then, we took real hot showers. We found a phone book in the room and looked for gemstone dealers in the business pages. In the early afternoon, we went out on the town for lunch and looking for gemstones.

First, we stopped into the local airline to see when I could get the next flight out for Trujillo, where my friend's the Zamora's had planned to meet me.

I had no idea what was happening because we already were 2 weeks overdue from my planned arrival there.

(one week waiting or the boat in Pucallpa and a week late in getting to Iquitos). There was no real way to call my friends back in Lima, so, I had to depend on the fate of the Gods and hope they would prevail in my favor.

Much to my astonishment, the lady at the small airline office told me there were no seats available for the next few days. It was only a once a day flight on a fifteen passenger plane that flew from Iquitos to Trujillo, a coastal town about 800 km North

West of Lima, framed by the Moche river which spills into the Pacific Ocean. It is home to the pre- historic Moche and Chimu (before the Incan conquest). Trujillo is where there is the famous ancient Incan adobe ruins of Chan Chan.

I learned that there would be stops in Tarapoto and Moyabamba (gateway towns to the Amazon region).

I love these mysterious names.

But this meant an all day trip with lots of up and down flying through the high altitude clouds and gusty mountain winds from the Andes.

Assignment 3.11.2015

…So now another delay and will I ever see the Zamora's again? Leo told me not to worry, it would all work out.

"Let's buy some gemstones," he said trying to change the subject and get my mind off of my worries.

We had a few names written on a piece of paper. We showed it to our taxi driver who was parked in front of the airline office and asked him to take us to the closest store. As we drove through the busy streets filled with people walking about, I sensed how different the pace of life was here than in Pucallpa.

Courtesy of Wikipedia.com

This was more of a "big time" town, although it was nowhere near the size in scale to any big city in the States or even Lima. Nowadays, the population is almost a half a million but back then maybe about 50,000. Even so, there still was a casual mood here, but it was a busy port town.

I was told by the Zamoras' son Miguel, an architect/civil engineer, to look at the mosaic tiles on the colonial buildings in Iquitos. So, I was noticing them here and there as we ventured through the side streets of town. There were very beautiful blue tones with intricate designs.

Courtesy of Wikipedia.com

Two days later, Leo and I took an historic tour of the city to see the remnants of what once was a thriving rich rubber- boom town at the turn of the Twentieth Century.

Abruptly, the taxi stopped by a modest sand colored building with a jewelry shop in the front. I noticed Leo was becoming more serious as our judgement day was approaching. We had to switch gears from our drinking days of chuchuhuasi to now our being gemstone buyers.

Leo knocked on the door. It was locked. After a few more knocks and a minute or two, a short man with a white shirt and black slacks with a pencil thin black moustache peeked through a peep hole, and then opened the door.

"Buenas dias," he offered.

"Si," Leo said with his Aussie accent.

We entered a small sparse office with a tiny glass top table bordered by a few simple wooden chairs.

Then, in broken English, the man said, "please, have a seat."

Leo and I looked at each other as if to say, our game is over. The man knows we are gringos.

"How can I help you?" the man spoke with his thin moustache wiggling.

I offered back in Spanish, *"Queremos piedras." Then in both Spanish and English, I repeated,"* Queremos semi-precious stones*. Como aqua marina."*

We didn't have to say anything more. The man went into his back office and after a minute or two returned with several trays filled with beautiful glimmering stones of various sizes shapes and colors.

Leo and I looked at each other as if to say, with dollar signs in our eyes, now we are in business. And Leo and I had to put on our best act to show the salesman that we knew what we were doing.

For more than an hour we looked at all the stones, held them up to the light and started to select a few from the many.

And now the classic game of how much to pay...

Assignment- 4/2/2015

Of course, we knew that we were lucky to get maybe a 10% or 15% discount, since we were about to spend maybe $800.00, ($400 each). But, nonetheless, we negotiated with our dealer and he did settle amicably on a discount.

Carefully, he packaged our goods. We had made what we thought was a fine selection of fifteen or so semi-precious aqua marine, topaz, smoky topaz, tourmaline, gemstones, some of which were large 3 or 4 karat sizes all beautifully cut.

We shook hands and Leo and I went on our merry way trying to contain our greedy smiles, thinking we were about to be rich with our new investment.

And now we were hungry, at least we thought so. We walked a little ways down the street, and came to a small restaurant. We promptly ordered the usual rice, beans and some fried plantains with river fish.

Our conversation then quickly turned to our futures. Leo was now excited thinking about fulfilling his dream of panning for gold in the Amazon. I was not so anxious to return to the States. Even though I was looking forward to starting my teaching job, in a way, I was wishing I could have gone into those orchid fields with Wild Bill or continue on with Leo and experience his adventures.

They had the thrill of the unknown lying ahead, while I felt I was going back to the same old familiar territory. The first time out of the States was feeling invigorating to my soul with all these fresh new images filled with different sounds, colors, smells, and exotic images.

Our heaping plate of food arrived. Leo and I both stared at the meal in a confused way. We hadn't seen so much food on a plate in a few weeks. Our stomachs growled with hunger and rejection because our bodies just couldn't absorb so much intake of food.

So, we just picked around our plates and ate what we could. When we were finished, we both put our paper napkins over the plates, a little embarrassed and not wanting to make the waiter feel we didn't enjoy the food.

The fried fish was delicious. Our first taste of fish even though we were on the river from Pucallpa to Iquitos. And my gums had stopped bleeding because of the sugar cane that my farmer friend had given me during the full moon night in the sugarcane fields.

After dinner, we walked some more down the streets. We looked around at the mixture of colonial remnants and simple buildings. Then, a nostalgic feeling set in that we had made this trip together, but that Leo and I would soon part company, wondering when we might ever see each other again.

We kept walking and walking, but as the darkness of night started to creep in, we decided to get back to our hotel and look again at our recently purchased treasures.

I remember there was a plaza with a little street fair and people strolling about. Everyone was in a relaxed mood.

There were vendors selling popcorn, nuts and a few musicians playing indigenous music on flutes and crude guitars. For a moment, Leo and I felt relaxed, but we were tired and anxious to get a taxi to take us back to our hotel.

When we arrived, we couldn't wait to open our neatly wrapped tiny parcel of gems. We sat on Leo's bed and unwrapped them placing each individual stone in front of us on a white hand towel. They seemed to glimmer and shine. Leo jubilantly tossed a few in the air and said, "We're rich."

Wild Bill always said that real stones would be cold and not warm to our breath. We tested them all and felt assured these gems were the real McCoy.

Our enthusiasm lasted only a few minutes. Then we bid each other "goodnight" and quickly fell asleep.

In the middle of the night, I started to dwell about my return to the States. It was all appearing very anti-climatic now. But first, I had to find the Zamora's, hopefully, still in Trujillo. Also, I did not write my parents all this time. They were probably wondering what ever happened to their son. But I wanted to experience my independence and allegiance to no one but myself. Yes, in hindsight, this would appear selfish. But this is where my head was…. And Leo, once again he seemed impervious to it all, as he snored in his deep sleep.

CHAPTER 4

THE RETURN

7/27/2016

My return to the States was a hard landing. The culture shock of re-entry from a world of jungle simplicity and individuality to my old world of conformity and expectations stirred deep feelings of anxiety within me.

Fall foliage was starting to reveal itself as I returned to Bellows Falls, Vermont at the end of August 1963, to begin my first year as a high school English teacher.

"Didn't think we'd ever see you again...welcome back," Mr. Holland, the Superintendent of Schools said with a certain sigh of relief, before the teacher's preschool conference began.

That day, I met three other teachers who would influence me greatly in the years to follow: Mary Toomey, Head of the English Department, Lou Celona, the Music teacher, and Edmund Brelsford, the French teacher. All three became great lifelong friends and well worth the emotional challenges of my return to meet them.

It was Labor Day weekend. School would start the next week. I didn't know anyone in my new community. It was a whole new world of experiences, sort of a new river trip. I felt fresh oxygen pouring into my blood and a sense of exhilaration. I was excited about what new experiences might lay ahead.

My self-imposed "year of Thoreau" began that weekend with long walks across the open fields and into the woods nearby my rented rustic cabin on the Westminster West Road about three miles out from the town of Saxtons River.

On Saturday, late in the afternoon, as I slowly entered into the pine scented forest on the west side from the hayfield, I sensed I was not alone. Abruptly, I stopped. Standing about 10 feet away directly in front of me, was a young deer about five feet tall. Its dark eyes stared straight through me as if to say, "Hello."

We both stood our ground, motionless.

Part of me was a little scared, of what I didn't know. Another part of me was curious but in awe of the pure spirit and innocence of this gentle yet untamed animal. We both stood in silent respect for each other for a minute. Who would flinch first? Suddenly, the deer turned away and quickly darted deeper into the womb of the woods, leaving me alone to meditate about this symbolic encounter.

Years later, when I researched the spiritual symbolism of deer, I read they are symbolic of true peace on Earth. Deer stimulate innocence and stir our poetic souls.

During the year in my cabin, I wrote my first book, POEMS. And now, I realize the deer was telling me in that brief moment, my time in Saxtons River was to be a year of reflective thought and writing.

The Bellows Falls Times article from February 13, 1964 said. "Local teacher publishes first volume of Poems. He makes use of a pre-Joycean stream of consciousness technique and takes delight in puns, some subtle, some obvious, a few Freudian but for the most part crafted for their sensuous not sensual shock.

The poet approaches the English language with the enthusiasm and inventiveness of a child gaining his first understanding of the new math. He is not afraid to make use of onomatopoeia, but certain of his susurrant symbols wisk across the reader's perception with the delicacy of lace.

Kramer uses his poems both to unveil and conceal emotions, some troubled, others light and amusing. As are all serious poets, he is absorbed with the inner, hidden conflict between good and evil, and takes advantage of an almost neo- Miltonian symbolism to express the good core of evil and the evil core of good."

My mind wandered back to the Amazon.

What a difference of scenery were the maple, birch, ash and evergreen pines, and spruce trees from the tropical jungle habitat along the Ucayali, not to mention the difference in climate from the humid heat to the now crispy cool Green Mountain air of Vermont.

In this solitude, I reflected as my DC-3 lifted off the runway and I looked down for the last time at Iquitos, the Amazon River and the Ucayali in the far distance. My thoughts turned rapidly like a movie in my mind to the variety of unique, one of a kind life experiences I had just encountered as I sat in the Governor's seat in the small airplane. How could I ever describe these special people and scenery? Did this mean anything to my former colleagues in law school or anyone I knew?

But yes, this moment in time did offer me the opportunity to experience a world I never knew existed. It opened up new channels of thoughts, which the study of the law, as I previously mentioned, was slowly suffocating, although I did like the intellectual debate in studying case law.

7/27/2016

Everything speeded up now as I swiftly made my way home to the States, where my final destination would be Washington, D.C. staying in Lima only a day before departing for the return. But first, my plane from Lima to Washington, D.C. stopped in Atlanta, GA.

In Atlanta, I stayed on the plane as passengers departed and new ones entered. Quickly, I noticed that I was about the only white person on the plane. I asked the gentleman sitting next to me if there was a convention or something happening in Washington, D.C..

He replied, "Don't you know what is happening?"

I said, "No. I've been out of the country for a while in the Amazon. What's happening?"

He responded," Today is The March on Washington with Martin Luther King."

"Oh," I replied not knowing what to really say as my mind was so far away from this return. It was August 28, 1963.

My body was tired and weary from all the travelling. I was still weak from the jungle diet, even though I was young now. just 22 and a half years old. I fell asleep wondering about my future and my recent past. Where is Rosita now and Leo? How do I ever return.

As the plane started its descent into Washington, I felt gloomy as though I was returning to the old familiar routine of law school. But then I realized this was no longer where I will be going. It's onto Vermont and teaching, a whole new experience and this lifted my spirits.

But there was now a burst of electric energy amongst the passengers on the plane. Some strong force was pulling them all together. I couldn't explain the feeling to myself, but something told me to follow the crowd to the Washington Monument and the Mall and experience The Great March on Washington.

Returning to my apartment near Dupont Circle, I threw my bags on the floor, took a quick shower, and then a cab close to the area where the march was taking place. All we could see were people, hundreds and hundreds and thousands of people all excited for their cause.

For some reason, I thought about my first trip to Florida from New Jersey by train about 1954. My father and mother took us there for Christmas vacation.

12/ 7/ 2015

I remember the overnight trains. We left Newark, New Jersey, about 12:30pm, after about an hour delay from New York City. My brother George and I shared a room. I got the top bed. The room was cool. We both had our own seat/sofa and could stare out the large window. And see all before us. After an hour my father took us to the lounge car. There were single plush chairs that swiveled. Other people were in the car and probably thought we were a bunch of wild cats but my father kept us in check, while my mother stayed in her room till dinner. George and I both had cokes and my father had his favorite scotch and soda.

At dinner we sat at our own table. The waiters all wore long black ties and a large white apron. The dinner, I still remember, as it was very comforting. I had meatloaf and mashed potatoes with green beans. Of course, for dessert I had vanilla ice cream with a little cookie.

After dinner we would all go back to the lounge car for a while before returning to our rooms for the night. George would cuddle into his bed and I into mine. I can still feel the train rolling on into the night. I remember at about midnight the train slowing down and coming into a station. I came down from my cubby hole and looked out the window. George was half awake. As the train came into the station-Rocky Mount, North Carolina, I saw for the first time in my life two signs. One said White and the other said Colored. I really didn't know the real significance until the next morning when I asked my father at breakfast to explain this situation.

Is this the United States of America where All people are created free and equal? Am I missing something?

And now, some 10 years later, Martin Luther King is preaching, "I Have a Dream."

A few days after the March on Washington I found my way home in Passaic, New Jersey. It was a Sunday about 1 o'clock. I smelled a barbecue coming from the backyard. I walked into the party and saw my mother. She was totally surprised because I had not told them of my return. We hugged and she cried, "I didn't know if I would ever see you again."

The following Sunday, after settling into my cabin in Vermont, I decided to attend the three different churches in the little town of Saxtons River to meet some of the families in the community where I would soon be teaching.

The choir music was wonderful in all three: the Catholic church, Methodist and Episcopal.

On Monday, as I walked through the school hallways, before classes started, I could hear some of the students mumble,

"That's Mr. Kramer, He's the new English teacher. He was in our Church yesterday."

The other student would reply," Oh no, he was in ours."

3/21/2017

Finally, my big moment arrived. I was an English teacher for real. Thank you Mr. Hall for your faith in me. Remember, it was you who recommended just a few short months ago that I should try this course of action.

Instead of walking into the classroom and standing in front of my senior class, I decided to sit in the back of the room

Most of the reason was insecurity on my part. The moment of truth had arrived. Did I have the courage to stand in front of these unknown students and have the ability to teach them anything? I had no formal teaching training. Although, I was a swim instructor at summer camp and Head of the waterfront as well as a camp counselor.

But now, I had to rely upon my mentors from 7 years of country day private school at Montclair Academy, particularly Mr. William Avery Barras and Mr. Frank Brogan, my English teachers. They trained us well. Every week in High School we wrote a theme paper of 500 words. Usually, we wrote about our interpretation of a question referring to our novel readings that week. But on this day, I was a young looking twenty -three - and-half- years old. Some of my students were older looking at eighteen. The class bell rang promptly at 8:15.

My students, sensing that no teacher had arrived, started to talk amongst themselves. They probably thought

I was a new student in town, even though I was wearing a sport coat and a tie sitting in the back row. These were country kids and wore simple clothes of jeans or khaki pants and plaid shirts. The girls wore skirts, sweaters and plain dresses.

After a few moments, the first spitball arrived shot from a student in the back row to a chap in the front row. Everyone laughed.

So, now I made my move and walked up to the blackboard. The disciplinarian in me took over my inner fears. I knew I had to establish order in the classroom.

Picking up a new piece of chalk, I wrote, "Mr. Kramer" in large letters. The class came to stiff attention. The spitball chap in the back of the class half yelled, "Geez Mr. Kramer, that's not fair. You were sitting here all this time." Everyone laughed.

Quickly, I replied, "Don't worry, I just wanted to get to know you all better." And with that, everyone gave a little sigh of relief. Mr. Kramer wasn't that bad after all.

I asked the class to turn their desks around and face the large single paned windows facing the outside world.

Our classroom was on the second floor. All we could see through the windows were the limbs and leaves of the sunlit autumn trees.

"Everyone, I want you to write a paper describing what you see through the windows." For the next 30 minutes the class of about, 28 students fell silent. The students scratched their hair, rubbed their chins, coughed, sneezed and sometimes wrote.

That night, I sat in my cabin at my desk and read the papers from my senior class. The moonlight shined through my cabin window as I concentrated with the silence of the woods. I couldn't believe I was now reading papers from my senior and four other classes. Only a few short years ago I was a student like them writing for Mr. Barras and Mr. Brogan. Whatever I learned would now be imparted to my students.

Basically, all of the senior class wrote just a few half sentences like "Look out window. See tree. See byrd."

"Wish I was the byrd so I culd flie a way. Not be in skool."

Some one else wrote, "Want go in army."

I realized then that these children had felt for a long time that the less they wrote, the less chance there would be to make a spelling or grammar mistake.

My mission now was to let them express themselves and not be so concerned with the rules of grammar or spelling, at least for now. This was to be my experiment.

I reflected on the young chap with the spitball incident and laughed to myself.

How could I really reprimand him, when only a few short years ago, I too shot a spitball in the lunchroom. I remember taking the straw from my milk carton and twisting one end into the side of the chocolate, strawberry and vanilla brick ice cream dessert.

Then, I shot the other end at my friend sitting across from me. However, he ducked. The ice cream missile flew past him and hit the French teacher, Mr. Adair, in his left eye as he was eating his spaghetti.

Wow, what a surprise. Mr. Adair looked around and was furious. He wiped his eye with his paper napkin. Then, he stood up and half yelled,"Who shot this spitball?"

Our code of silence went into effect. Everyone around me was trying as hard as could be to muffle their laughter.

When no one answered, "Alright," Mr. Adair said furiously. "Detention for everyone. 30 minutes after school, everyone report here."

4/1/2017

My head nodding and wobbling up and down suddenly woke me up from a deep slumber at my desk. Some of the papers had dropped to the floor. The silence of the woods was eerie, but peaceful. I opened the creaky cabin door and stood on the top of three well- worn, uneven wooden plank steps. Taking a deep breathe of the pure mountain air I stared at the moonbeams flaring across the open road from where the deer lived. Tree limbed shadows cast sketches as the leaves whispered in the cool night air. It felt like 3 a.m., but it was only about 11 o'clock. I felt secure in my isolation a few miles from town. My neighbor, farmer Arthur Beamis who was also the school bus driver and his wife lived just down the road.

To my right, I stared down the dirt road seeing my nearest neighbor's cabin about 50 yards away, tucked around the bend of the narrow dirt roadway. The cabin was mostly hidden by some maple trees and pine, a simple cabin, elf-like with a high-pitched roof, missing wooden siding with patches of tar paper showing. Their wood burning stove sent smoke signals into the evening sky and brought a comforting cozy smell to my solitude on the Westminister West road- I was not alone.

Yesterday, I had made an arrangement with Mr. Allen, of the Allen Brothers Orchard for his young son, about 10- years-old, to deliver two five- gallon jugs of water to my cabin every morning at 6 a.m. The deal was I would pay the lad 5 cents a gallon. That was 70 cents a week. It was big money back then. My salary for the school year was $4,000, plus $50 for directing the senior play and $50 for being advisor to the school yearbook. Amazingly, at the end of the year I saved $2,000 from this modest salary. My expenses were very few. My rent was 80 dollars a month. I needed the water jugs because the water table was very low after the summer dry season, and the pipes froze in the winter. I took my showers in the high school gym most of the time.

Mr. Allen, who left school after the 8th grade to work in the family orchard, was very proud to have his son deliver the water to the new English teacher in town.

The temperature on my long outside thermometer read a crisp 42. A frost was laying down in the meadow. As I turned to enter back into my warm cabin, my thoughts also turned to Leo and the Amazon. Where was he now? Was he well?

Did he find any gold? He said he would write to me.

Meantime, my mother was contacting a friend in New York city who knew a diamond dealer to find out what our gemstones might be worth. What was Rosita doing? I miss all my new friends who I might never see again.

What was Vitor Raul of Yarinacochina doing? It was enough thinking for one day. It was time for me to go to bed.

4/11/2017

The next day, I woke up to a clunking sound at my side doorway steps.

It must be 6 a.m. My two five - gallon water jugs just arrived. As I lay in bed, the chirping from the birds welcomed the early morning dew.

I briefly thought about what I might say to my students on this my second day of class. The shower water was cold but it woke me up.

The countryside drive to school was a bucolic masterpiece; a winding two lane country road downhill passing by farmer Beamis' Victorian house. He had just finished milking his five cows before driving the school bus parked in his driveway. I gave a beep to him and he waved back with a friendly smile. Then I drove through a flat open meadow field where a second crop of hay was about to be harvested. Around the next bend on the right was a big cow barn with well worn weathered red\paint and a huge manure pile beside it. I remember one

Saturday, a few weeks later, I saw an artist sitting by the side of the road by her easel, painting this scene. I had stopped my car and walked to the artist to observe what she was painting. After saying hello, I asked if I could see her rendering. It was a very accurate facsimile of the scene.

Then the big burly farmer with well-worn Osh Gosh jeans, soiled and dirtied by his sweat and hard toil, walked by and took a look. He grinned at the painting and saw the manure pile on the canvass next to the barn. He said," Looks pretty gooood, but it ain't got the smell." We all laughed.

But for now, on the way to my second day of class, I continued past the manure pile barn and into the open stretch of farmland approaching the hamlet of Saxtons River. I lived about five miles from town. Nurtured by the waterpower, the town formed in 1783. Through the years there were some textile mills, tannery, distillery, gristmill, and a large Inn on the main street that began in 1803. Also, it is the home of Vermont Academy established in 1876.

As I approached the little bridge crossing the narrow rapid river, Tenney's lumber mill was on my left. The aromatic smell of freshly sawed pine boards permeated through my open car window reminding me of my family's lumberyard in New Jersey.

Here in this gentle bucolic countryside, this familiar scent made me feel at home with my boyhood when I unloaded the box cars full of Georgia and Carolina pine…and all those 2 x 4's and 2 x 6's etc., I helped unload when the school year ended and before my brother and I went to summer camp in New Hampshire in the months of July and August.

It was 7:15, as I passed by Tenney's and already there was some activity with a few workers walking about. Large pile of logs lay in front of the mill by the road.

Near the roadside, a truck full of logs was sitting and waiting to be unloaded.

Turning right after the bridge onto the main street of town, I noticed the Post Office where I had to go to register a box to collect my mail later today after school. My thoughts turned again to Leo. I wondered when and if I would receive a letter from the jungle and hear of his exotic gold seeking adventures.

My new life nestled in this protective quaint Vermont world seemed so tame and safe compared to Leo's life in the unknown treachery of the unexplored Amazon.

After the Post Office on the left was a large building which later I learned was the Saxtons River Inn. Parked to the side of the building was a fleet of about a dozen Cadillac cars, black and grey, the round turtle like sedan ones circa 1940's Series 61.My curiosity was aroused. I knew I had to check this scene out, perhaps later today after school, and after I open my new Post Office box. But now I had another 12 miles to drive to the school.

When I entered my senior class with the theme papers I had read the night before, I had a certain trepidation as to how best to tell these students that I wanted to suspend all grammar and spelling rules for a while and that I was more interested in what their feelings were about and what they observed.

They appeared a bit confused when I told them this. But they really liked the idea of no grades for spelling or grammar mistakes.

One of the students blurted out, "So what are we going to write about next Mr. Kramer?"

I replied, "tell me what you did this summer."

For the next thirty minutes everyone put their heads down and seemed to concentrate and think but wrote very little yet a bit more than the first day.

At the end of class, when they were turning in their papers, one of the students asked, "What did you do this summer Mr. Kramer?"

A bit startled, as though I had almost forgotten, I replied,   I was in the Amazon jungle in Peru. Do you know where that is?"

Their eyes were in awe, filled with curiosity. "I'll tell you more about it tomorrow," And so my great summer adventure continued as each day forward I would tell them a little about my trip on the Ucayali and my friendship with Leo. We all waited expectantly for his first letter from somewhere.

The students continued to write their thoughts, a little more each day. Of course, the spelling and grammar errors were a constant. But I felt I opened their minds to reveal their souls.

Maybe English class isn't so boring as they read their papers out loud and began to learn about each other. Also, those who were a little shy at first began liking to talk about themselves and gained a certain confidence in public speaking. I too was amazed at myself, that I was influential in helping these children to express themselves.

One day, in the teacher's lounge where we gathered during our breaks, Mary Toomey, the Head of the English Department asked me in her brisk but friendly tone and twinkling blue eyes, " So what are you teaching your students, Frederick?"

I answered," I have no idea, but we're having fun!"

Her grin showed me she understood…

A few weeks later, I told this senior class,

"Everyone stand up and be quiet. We are going to walk out of the school and go downtown to Main Street. No talking when we leave class now and walk through the hallways."

They were amazed that I would take everyone out of school at 8:30 in the morning on a Tuesday during the week.

We walked single file out of the school down the multiple steps into the fresh autumn air. I could sense everyone felt reborn with freedom. We are out of school and beginning an adventure. Where is Mr. Kramer taking us?

The class walked down five blocks to Main Street. We first walked into the coffee shop and said hello to the counter waitress. Next stop we walked into The Model Press which was a few doors down the street. After saying hello to Dave, the owner, and his wife, we then walked across the street to the Bellows Falls diner and then to Fletcher's stationery store. We spent about ten minutes there and walked out. Then we walked past the movie theatre where the graduation is held in June. Then our final walk was back to school. Everyone was a little tired from our early morning walk. I told them that tomorrow they would write a paper about what they saw and learned. Hopefully, this time it would be more than a few sentences. Time will tell.

CHAPTER 5

BELLOWS FALLS

I really didn't know anything about Bellows Falls, Vermont, before I started teaching school there. I was hired on the spot during my interview with Superintendent Mr. Holland and the Principal Mr. Davis, and then I quickly raced on down to the Amazon.

Now that I returned for the school year, the reality of this being my new home started to set in. Usually, after school, I would cruise downtown a few blocks from School street to explore the neighborhood.

I would go down a little steep hill in my 1954 Ford Fairlane which I bought from one of my students, Ray Plante, for 40 dollars. It was a bit rusty and faded green but I didn't care because it was cheap transportation. Also, it reminded me of my teenage years when I would either walk or take my Schwinn bike to Third Ward park a few blocks from my house.

This was 1954-1958 and I was only a teenager. Usually, on Saturday mornings the park was filled with friends and many other boys and girls from all over town. It was quite the scene. Some of the "hot shot" seniors who could drive sat in their

Ford Fairlanes with tops down sometimes hugging their babes who would flaunt their "prize" in front of their girlfriends like real showoffs.

Along the main drag of Passaic Avenue bordering the ballpark there was a long line of other types of cars like Chevy's, Mercury's, big fin Chryslers, Studebakers, DeSotos, Packards, Pontiac Bonnevilles' and Nash Ramblers all shined up.

Tom Saba with his hot dog truck parked at the far end near the Erie Lackawana train station. He also sold popcorn, popsicles and my favorite orange creamsicles. If I remember correctly, a hot dog cost 25 cents with sauerkraut. Tom always served them with a smile. He was like a favorite Uncle to all of us.

Most of us guys combed our hair either in a ducktail like Elvis or the Fonz. The girls wore bobby socks and bright white sneakers that never seemed to have a scuffmark. Many of the girls wore white pleated skirts with a sweatshirt or sweater. Of course in the hot weather they wore tee shirts which thrilled the boys. I didn't wonder why?

Who would know that 10 years later I would be in Bellows Falls, Vermont, which sat on the riverbanks of the graceful, long winding Connecticut River. It was only a few moments before, in my teenage years that I used to canoe on overnight camping trips from my New Hampshire summer camp. We would put our metal canoes in the water at Hanover by Dartmouth College. Then we would set out on a three or four day voyage downstream along the gentle Vermont farmland roaming with dairy cows and open hayfields and forests. Occasionally, large loud barking dogs would sometimes run down to the riverbank to scare us off and drink the refreshing water during the lazy hot summer days.

We would eventually end the trip in Thetford, Vermont. But those nurturing idyllic experiences still to this day provide me with a comfort zone of youthful innocence and a time to reflect with no cares in the world.

I remember we would just jump out of the canoes to swim in the slow moving current and pull the canoes alongside us.The river water was warm on the top foot or two where the humid hot summer sun reflected down from the cloudless blue sky above. Diving under the warm upper level my body suddenly shivered from the cold fresh water waiting below. The current moved slowly but continuously. The dark color made me feel like I was in outer space and all alone. It was scary like being in a haunted house and you didn't know if you would ever get out. Your mind plays tricks and if you let it wander you start to worry if you will ever see the surface again. I held my breath for about a minute before I would quickly swim upward towards the warm comfortable level finally returning to earth surfacing with a fish like splash. With great relief I would blow out any water in my mouth and take deep breaths of air to refill my lungs with new energy.

We would always look around to see if our buddies had made it back to the surface as well. Our counselor would ask for a buddy call to check if everyone was accounted for. So, we all had a number and would shout out loud, "1,2,3,4,5,6,7,8, etc.," until he was certain everyone was there.

Our next struggle was to get back into the canoes. One person would hold the back end of the canoe while the other chap would struggle his way up into the canoe and then kick his way into an awkward position. With a sigh of relief, I would sigh and shout to my buddy, "Your turn now!"

We would sing songs like "100 Bottles of Beer on the Wall" to pass the time and hear our echoes rebounding above the shimmering relentless sunlight skirting off the rambling water.

But now, my life has changed. I have responsibilities. I am a teacher, and responsible for 5 classes and almost 150 students plus advisor to the Yearbook and Director of the Senior play.

Bellows Falls had an interesting past.

It was the end of the logging run at the turn of the century. The last major drive was in 1915.

And now, I am here for real in Bellows Falls and have the whole year ahead of me. My mind turned to Leo and I wondered what was happening to him. Did he find any gold? What conditions was he living? Was he ok?

Before you knew it, I was back in Saxtons River. After getting a new P.O. Box I decided to go to the house where I was told at the Post Office that is where Major Angus lived, the man with many cars. The rest became history-our history.

My first encounter with the Major was with his long time Secretary Lillian. I asked if the Major was home. She replied he was resting. At that precise moment, the voice from upstairs boomed down, "Who is there?"

We both looked startled and Miss Lily replied, "Mr. Kramer."

"I'll be right down." And that is how we began our relationship.

"I'm the new high school English teacher in Bellows Falls. I live out on the Westminster West road a few miles from town."

"You can sit here if you wish, Mr. Kramer."

As I sat I looked around the large room which was all filled with papers and papers and papers. Within a minute, the Major started walking down the stairs. He was somewhat smaller than my height but definitely had a larger stomach, and about 30 years older.

As he thudded to the bottom stair, he replied, "And a good afternoon to you kind sir. What is your name?"

I added, "Fred Kramer, sir."

"You want some scotch?"

I hesitated for a moment. And then quickly replied, "Why not!"

And so it all began.

As the year unfolded, I would meet with the Major at least 2 or 3 times a week. Sometimes, we would just sit in his large room with Lillian and talk as she did her work. Some other moments were filled with amusement as we would get into one of his Cadillac cars and zoom off to the Alstead Country Club, about 20 miles away, where he loved to play golf. But we had another mission.

I was his younger playmate and would stand on the putting green and do what I was told to do by him. Sometimes he would tell me to hold my shoulders to the left and the golf club to the right. After thinking for a minute he would then ask me to shift my position.

We would proceed like this week after week, after which we would have a scotch and a cigar at the country club and I would listen to the Major philosophize and meander with his thoughts. Once in a while he would treat me to a hamburger, which meant he had some other things he wanted to talk about.

All in all I learned to be obedient but at the same time I was also learning to be a student of this very unusual person. The more I knew him the more he told me about his wisdom with the stock market and his bi-monthly newsletter. He also revealed how he was friends at school with Winston Churchill.

About a month later, I walked into the principal's office at school to ask a question and the secretary said, "Oh, Mr. Kramer, here is a letter for you."

"Really," I replied. Looking at the letter I did not recognize it at first. But then I knew who it was from-Leo! I hurried to my first class.

When this senior class began I immediately announced I had a letter from Leo in the Amazon.

"What did he say?" they all asked – excitedly!

"I don't know . Let's see" And so we read the letter.

Leo mailed the letter from a town in Colombia almost one month ago, but here it is. He said that he was ok. He was gearing up for a first try into the jungle with a new buddy he met in the town. Of course he wanted to know what was happening with our semi-precious stone investment. We all sat back into our chairs a little bit relieved.

But then he asked if nothing was happening he would prefer to get his $400 back. Now everyone sat back in their chairs and looked at me to see my response.

"What are you going to tell him Mr. Kramer?" One of the female students asked.

I didn't know what to say so I muttered, "I'll think about it."

And so all day I talked about my letter from Leo to my other classes- five in all.

That night I thought about what I wanted to write to Leo. So many thoughts, so many ideas. But, at last I wrote him and told him my mother was trying to show the collection to a dealer in New York city. If she didn't find out anything in the next two weeks I could send him his money back. Otherwise, I was curious about his life. I dropped the paper and fell asleep.

The next afternoon after school I dashed back to Saxtons River to the post office and mailed the letter hoping it will arrive sooner than later.

I always wondered what would happen to Leo. But, I couldn't do anything about it now. Time rolled on.. And before you knew it, a month rolled by and one day at my Saxtons River post office I had another letter from Leo. It was a Saturday morning. So, I sat in my car and read what he had to say.

It seems like he had gone into the jungle with his friend and after a few weeks they did not have much luck. They were going to try another spot in two weeks and he wanted me to send his money back to him.

My mother in the meantime had written and informed me that there has been a big rush of these gems and they were not worth much more than what we bought them for. On Monday I went to the bank after school and withdrew $400 plus a bonus of $200 extra for good luck. Of course, I told my classes about this communication and what I had done.

Now I felt Leo's life and mine were separating.

Winter was not too far away. Thanksgiving was only ten days from now. And I was beginning to write my book of POEMS. And soon Leo will have his money- I hope.

The days rolled on, Thanksgiving came and went, except for one major interruption- the assassination of President John F. Kennedy. The whole world stood silent. The day of his funeral I sat in the living room of my neighbors, the Beamis's. We talked about the future and their past lives. Mrs. Beamis made some home-made cupcakes. They were delicious. I can still taste them today. However, it was only a few days before and I was teaching school about 2 in the afternoon. There was an announcement from Mr. Davis, the school principal. He said that President

Kennedy was shot and killed. School was cancelled and we should go home and pray. My class filed out silently. The school became left in silence and everyone was in a state of shock. Life as we knew it stopped. The whole world was stunned. President Kennedy had left a definite impression on us all.

On the following Monday, I was asked by one of my male students, "Where are you going to be at Christmas, Mr. Kramer?"

I didn't have any plans yet. I just answered, "I'll be around, just travelling around."

Christmas and the New Year came and went. Life moved forward and soon it was February. Every week my students would ask me, "Where's Leo, Mr. Kramer?"

I didn't really have an answer for them, I didn't know. We all were concerned because now it has been a few months since our last conversation. But one day just before the end of February 1964, I had a letter in my mailbox from someone I didn't know from Australia. I waited until I returned home to read it-one of the saddest letters I ever read.

The letter was from Leo's sister in Melbourne, Mrs. Karakens. She wrote to tell me personally that she found my letters in Leo's knapsack. She figured we were very close and wanted to tell me the news.

Leo was sick in the jungle. But he managed to find his way back to Quito, Ecuador. He was in a room at a rooming house being treated for Polio. For several weeks they tried to cure him but he was too weak and died.

The rest of the day and night all I could think about was Leo and the short but lifetime experiences we shared together on the Ucayali. And now almost sixty years later, I still reflect on our memories. Time is strange.

I wrote a poem – A FRIEND.

Although he was my elder
he was my friend
to walk with, to talk with, to live to learn to talk with,
to live
to learn.

One day I was told
I would not walk with him Again
And yet
today
I have
a friend.

That night I didn't sleep. All I could do was think and remember all the times Leo and I shared for a couple of weeks.

The next morning as I drove to school all I could do was think about was my students and what would be their reaction to this somber news. As it turned out, all of my classes were totally devastated by this sad news. We all were looking forward to meeting Leo. And yet, in our own individual ways, we did meet him.

Who knows what our life fortunes will be. All we can do is proceed onward and hope for the best. I never thought my relationship with Leo would end this way. But here, some 60 years later I still think about him all the time-and Rosita.

Strange how one river has such a strong influence on you – the Ucayali. And now it is the Connecticut river. For several months I wrestled with the loss of Leo, as did my students. It seemed that we were all cheated from getting to know Leo. But such is life. We all must plan for the unknown and the unexpected.

My experiences on the Ucayali never ended, as I still always think about my moments there. Now my life has many dreams yet to be fulfilled. Who would know at this point that I would be married in two years and living in New York City? Who knew that after ten years I would have three sons? I would be selling Rolls Royce cars and being a Fine Art dealer and an Art Publisher? Who knew that I would be in Brazil, having a television show, some twenty years later and divorced.

But in the meantime, I was living a life in Vermont and experiencing the four seasons for the first time in my young life in this beautiful state. I had many new friends and was finishing my first book of POEMS. What else could I want at this time except to be with my on again-off again girlfriend who was studying in Madrid, Spain. I decided for spring break to travel there but first I would go to London and offer my book of POEMS for sale, which was about to be printed at The Model Press in Bellows Falls.

I wasn't going to tell her that I was coming because I thought this would add some romance. Additionally, I had received a letter from the Draft Board informing me that I was drafted and to report immediately. But Mr. Holland, my superintendent, had written to the Draft Board requesting a deferment until June 1964. This was in the beginning of the Vietnam War. So, there was a lot of confusion going on in my life which also distracted me from thinking about Leo, although now I wish I was with him searching for gold in the Amazon. Maybe this was just an escape from my current reality but it never happened.

Who knew at this time what will be? But I was off to London and Spain for the first time in my life, and so life goes...and so life goes on!

Printed in the United States
By Bookmasters